D0579661

CHRISTMAS GREETINGS
FROM THE
PRESIDENTS

The White House with the National Christmas Tree. (Shutterstock/Orhan Cam)

CHRISTMAS GREETINGS
FROM THE
PRESIDENTS

SHADOW
MOUNTAIN

Special thanks to Jana Erickson

Presidential portraits courtesy the Executive Office of the President of the United States, public domain.

© 2016 Shadow Mountain Publishing

Visit us at ShadowMountain.com

Library of Congress Cataloging-in-Publication Data
Title: Christmas greetings from the presidents.
Description: Salt Lake City, Utah : Shadow Mountain, [2016] | ©2016 |
    Includes bibliographical references.
Identifiers: LCCN 2016008704 | ISBN 9781629722207 (hardbound : alk. paper)
Subjects: LCSH: Presidents—United States—Messages. | Christmas—United States. | United States—Politics and
    government. | LCGFT: Speeches.
Classification: LCC J81.4 .C47 2016 | DDC 352.23/8—dc23
LC record available at http://lccn.loc.gov/2016008704

Printed in China
RR Donnelley, Shenzhen, China

10   9   8   7   6   5   4   3   2   1

Contents

Introduction

    Christmas is a time for reflection and renewal, for family and faith, and Americans have long celebrated the holiday with joy and charity. Tradition holds that Alabama was the first state to recognize Christmas as an official state holiday in 1836 (Oklahoma was last in 1907), but it wasn't until June 28, 1870, that Christmas was declared a federal holiday.

    In 1923, the White House began a tradition of lighting the "National Community Christmas Tree," and in 1927, President Calvin Coolidge gave a short message to the American people. Every Christmas since then, the President of the United States has delivered a holiday message to the nation. Some of the messages have been long, others have been short, but they all have expressed a desire for Americans to find "peace on earth" and encouraged us to extend "good will to men."

    Gathered in this volume are selections from at least one of the Christmas messages from each president since Coolidge. Alongside those presidential messages is a brief historical note that offers us a glimpse into the history unfolding at that time. For example, what President Franklin D. Roosevelt said during Christmas 1941 is made even more poignant knowing that the attack on Pearl Harbor had happened just weeks earlier. Likewise, one of President Ronald Reagan's Christmas messages is even more impressive knowing that the Iron Curtain was about to come down.

Each of these historic and inspirational messages from the presidents of the United States are filled with the spirit of Christmas and remind us that both patriotism and faith in God have a place in our holiday celebrations.

The White House in 1929. (Library of Congress)

1927

The Tradition Begins
CALVIN COOLIDGE

HISTORICAL NOTE: *In 1923, during the first year of President Calvin Coolidge's administration, the tradition of a National Community Christmas Tree was established in the nation's capital. In a Christmas Eve tree-lighting ceremony held that year on the Ellipse, President Coolidge was present to illuminate the 3,000 light bulbs adorning a balsam fir from his native state of Vermont. Tragically, that year would be the last Christmas the Coolidge family would celebrate together, as their sixteen-year-old son, also named Calvin, died the following July. While the country basked in a period of peace and prosperity, Mrs. Coolidge later noted that the president was never the same after their son's death. Although the tradition of a national tree-lighting ceremony was quickly embraced by the American public, it was not until 1927 that President Coolidge, sometimes called "Silent Cal,"*

1923 National Community Christmas Tree showing the Ellipse in the background. (Library of Congress)

offered the first official presidential Christmas greeting to the country. That year this brief handwritten message from President Coolidge appeared on Christmas Day in major newspapers throughout the country.

Christmas is not a time or a season but a state of mind. To cherish peace and good will, to be plenteous in mercy, is to have the real spirit of Christmas. If we think on these things there will be born in us a Savior and over us all will shine a star— sending its gleam of hope to the world. (Calvin Coolidge, "Christmas Greeting to the Nation," December 15, 1927.)

In 1954, the annual tree lighting celebration that began during President Calvin Coolidge's term in office became the "Christmas Pageant of Peace," a three-week long winter festival and a tradition that continues today.

President and Mrs. Coolidge at the Christmas Eve lighting ceremony of the first National Community Christmas Tree. (Library of Congress)

1929
Depression Years
HERBERT HOOVER

HISTORICAL NOTE: America's thirty-first president took office in 1929, the year the stock market crashed and the country plummeted into the Great Depression. Ironically, the man who had gained wide recognition as a great humanitarian in the aftermath of World War I bore much of the public blame for the country's economic crisis. Many felt that he had failed to recognize the severity of the situation, and he was broadly viewed as callous and insensitive to the suffering of the masses.

While President Hoover did not mention the economy in his brief Christmas greeting to the nation that year—the first year that a presidential Christmas message was broadcast by radio—it is interesting to note that his Christmas greeting to disabled veterans a few days earlier focused on remembering the contribution of those who had served their country in the past.

President and Mrs. Hoover on White House porch, 1929. (Library of Congress)

⌒

May I have the privilege of wishing you all, and the great unseen audience, both a merry Christmas and a most happy new year? (Herbert Hoover, "Christmas Greeting to the Nation," December 24, 1929.)

⌒

To all disabled ex-service men and women:

I send you cordial Christmas greetings and my best wishes for your happiness in the new year, and I do pray for your restoration to health. Your country has not forgotten you and will not forget. The Nation's pride in your valor and devotion, and

During a Christmas Eve party in 1929, an electrical fire broke out in the West Wing of the White House. While Mrs. Hoover kept the party going, the president was called away from the festivities and watched as the Oval Office was gutted in the blaze.

its gratitude for the service you have rendered, are manifest in its continued concern for your welfare and in its warm sympathy and regard for you. (Herbert Hoover, "Christmas Message to Disabled Veterans," December 20, 1929.)

The scene at the Executive Offices of the White House during the fire on December 24, 1929. (Library of Congress)

1933

"The Happiest of Christmases"
FRANKLIN D. ROOSEVELT

HISTORICAL NOTE: America's longest-serving president celebrated his first Christmas in the White House in 1933. With the despair of the Depression years still fresh in the public's memory, he spoke at the National Christmas Tree Lighting Ceremony about embracing a culture of charity, compassion, and service, and of 1933 as "the happiest of Christmases." But while the economy slowly improved, by the end of his first term in office, world politics had deteriorated and war was once again on the horizon.

We in the Nation's capital are gathered around this symbolic tree celebrating the coming of Christmas; in spirit we join with millions of others, men and women and children, throughout our own

Workmen in 1937 decorate the National Christmas Tree in preparation for its lighting by President Roosevelt. (Library of Congress)

land and in other countries and continents, in happy and reverent observance of the spirit of Christmas.

For me and for my family it is the happiest of Christmases.

To the many thousands of you who have thought of me and have sent me greetings, and I hope all of you are hearing my voice, I want to tell you how profoundly grateful I am. If it were within my power so to do I would personally thank each and every one of you for your remembrance of me, but there are so many thousands of you that that happy task is impossible.

Even more greatly, my happiness springs from the deep conviction that this year marks a greater national understanding of the significance in our modern lives of the teachings of Him whose birth we celebrate. To more and more of us the words "Thou shalt love thy neighbor as thyself" have taken on a meaning that is showing itself and proving itself in our purposes and daily lives.

May the practice of that high ideal grow in us all in the year to come.

I give you and send you one and all, old and young, a Merry Christmas and a truly Happy New Year.

And so, for now and for always "God Bless Us Every One."

(Franklin D. Roosevelt, "A Christmas Greeting to the Nation," December 24, 1933.)

President Roosevelt speaks at the lighting of the National Christmas Tree in 1933. (Library of Congress)

President Roosevelt typically entertained his family on Christmas Eve with an annual reading of Charles Dickens's *A Christmas Carol*. Following the annual dramatic rendering, each member of the family was invited to hang his or her stocking on the mantel in the President's bedroom. The First Lady would fill the stockings late that night in readiness for Christmas morning.

1941
A World at War
FRANKLIN D. ROOSEVELT

HISTORICAL NOTE: Within weeks of the Japanese attack on Pearl Harbor, President Roosevelt delivered this stirring Christmas message at the National Christmas Tree Lighting Ceremony on December 24, 1941. A few days earlier, Prime Minister Winston Churchill had secretly crossed the Atlantic at great personal risk to meet with President Roosevelt. To the surprise of the American public, the two leaders spoke together from the balcony of the White House at the Christmas Eve celebration. In a program broadcast by radio across the world, they spoke about the importance of observing Christmas "with all of its memories and all of its meanings," despite the uncertainties and gloom of war which lay ahead.

Fellow workers for freedom:

There are many men and women in America—sincere and faithful men and women—who are asking themselves this Christmas:

How can we light our trees? How can we give our gifts?

How can we meet and worship with love and with uplifted spirit and heart in a world at war, a world of fighting and suffering and death?

How can we pause, even for a day, even for Christmas Day, in our urgent labor of arming a decent humanity against the enemies which beset it?

Four generations of Roosevelts gathered for a family Christmas at the White House. (National Archives)

How can we put the world aside, as men and women put the world aside in peaceful years, to rejoice in the birth of Christ?

These are natural—inevitable—questions in every part of the world which is resisting the evil thing.

And even as we ask these questions, we know the answer. There is another preparation demanded of this Nation beyond and beside the preparation of weapons and materials of war. There is demanded also of us the preparation of our hearts; the arming of our hearts. And when we make ready our hearts for the labor and the suffering and the ultimate victory which lie ahead, then we observe Christmas Day—with all of its memories and all of its meanings—as we should.

Looking into the days to come, I have set aside a day of prayer, and in that Proclamation I have said:

"The year 1941 has brought upon our Nation a war of aggression by powers

---

At President Roosevelt's request, 1941 was the first year that the National Christmas Tree was positioned on the grounds of the White House. Unbeknownst to all, it would be the last time President Roosevelt would push the button to light the National Christmas Tree. While the tradition continued, the tree remained unlit for the next four years due to wartime conservation of electricity and blackout restrictions. Chimes were hung in place of lights and area schoolchildren collected old and new ornaments to help decorate the tree.

dominated by arrogant rulers whose selfish purpose is to destroy free institutions. They would thereby take from the freedom-loving peoples of the earth the hard-won liberties gained over many centuries.

"The new year of 1942 calls for the courage and the resolution of old and young to help to win a world struggle in order that we may preserve all we hold dear.

"We are confident in our devotion to country, in our love of freedom, in our inheritance of courage. But our strength, as the strength of all men everywhere, is of greater avail as God upholds us.

"Therefore, I . . . do hereby appoint the first day of the year 1942 as a day of prayer, of asking forgiveness for our shortcomings of the past, of consecration to the tasks of the present, of asking God's help in days to come.

"We need His guidance that this people may be humble in spirit but strong in the conviction of the right; steadfast to endure sacrifice, and brave to achieve a victory of liberty and peace."

Our strongest weapon in this war is that conviction of the dignity and brotherhood of man which Christmas Day signifies—more than any other day or any other symbol.

Against enemies who preach the principles of hate and practice them, we set our faith in human love and in God's care for us and all men everywhere.

It is in that spirit, and with particular thoughtfulness of those, our sons and brothers, who serve in our armed forces on land and sea, near and far—those who serve for us and endure for us that we light our Christmas candles now across the continent from one coast to the other on this Christmas Eve.

President Franklin D. Roosevelt and Prime Minister Winston Churchill on the South Portico of the White House during the National Christmas Tree Lighting Ceremony. (Franklin D. Roosevelt Presidential Library)

We have joined with many other Nations and peoples in a very great cause. Millions of them have been engaged in the task of defending good with their life-blood for months and for years.

One of their great leaders stands beside me. He and his people in many parts of the world are having their Christmas trees with their little children around them, just as we do here. He and his people have pointed the way in courage and in sacrifice for the sake of little children everywhere.

And so I am asking my associate, my old and good friend, to say a word to the people of America, old and young, tonight. Winston Churchill, Prime Minister of Great Britain.

(Franklin D. Roosevelt, "Christmas Eve Message to the Nation," December 24, 1941.)

1944

"The Christmas Spirit Lives"

FRANKLIN D. ROOSEVELT

HISTORICAL NOTE: Throughout 1944, the Allied forces made significant gains on many fronts throughout Europe. For a war-weary nation who had given so much in the pursuit of victory, the prospects for peace seemed closer than at any other point in the previous three years. The White House Christmas cards that year were imprinted with the greeting: "With Christmas Greetings and our best wishes for a Happier Nineteen Forty-Five." President Roosevelt died just four months later, on April 12, 1945. Although the war wasn't over, the "new day of peace on Earth" for which the President had prayed in his final Christmas address was very near.

It is not easy to say "Merry Christmas" to you, my fellow Americans, in this time of destructive war.

Nor can I say "Merry Christmas" lightly tonight to our armed forces at their battle stations all over the world—or to our allies who fight by their side.

Here, at home, we will celebrate this Christmas Day in our traditional American way—because of its deep spiritual meaning to us; because the teachings of Christ are fundamental in our lives; and because we want our youngest generation to grow up knowing the significance of this tradition and the story of the coming of the immortal Prince of Peace and Good Will. But, in perhaps every home in the United States, sad and anxious thoughts will be continually with the millions of our loved ones who are suffering hardships and misery, and who are risking their very lives to preserve for us and for all mankind the fruits of His teachings and the foundations of civilization itself.

Franklin D. Roosevelt delivered his 1943 and 1944 Christmas messages on the radio from his study in Hyde Park, New York. (Franklin D. Roosevelt Presidential Library)

The Christmas spirit lives tonight in the bitter cold of the front lines in Europe and in the heat of the jungles and swamps of Burma and the Pacific islands. Even the roar of our bombers and fighters in the air and the guns of our ships at sea will not drown out the messages of Christmas which come to the hearts of our fighting

In 1944, President Roosevelt's Christmas gift to his staff was a reproduction of the D-Day Prayer, which he had originally issued on the evening of the invasion of Normandy and read to the nation over the radio on June 6, 1944. The President also had the prayer made into a slip-cased, limited edition book as a gift for his close friends.

men. The thoughts of these men tonight will turn to us here at home around our Christmas trees, surrounded by our children and grandchildren and their Christmas stockings and gifts—just as our own thoughts go out to them, tonight and every night, in their distant places.

We all know how anxious they are to be home with us, and they know how anxious we are to have them—and how determined every one of us is to make their day of homecoming as early as possible. And—above all—they know the determination of all right-thinking people and Nations, that Christmases such as those that we have known in these years of world tragedy shall not come again to beset the souls of the children of God.

This generation has passed through many recent years of deep darkness, watching the spread of the poison of Hitlerism and Fascism in Europe—the growth of imperialism and militarism in Japan—and the final clash of war all over the world. Then came the dark days of the fall of France, and the ruthless bombing of England, and the desperate battle of the Atlantic, and of Pearl Harbor and Corregidor and Singapore.

Since then the prayers of good men and women and children the world over have been answered. The tide of battle has turned, slowly but inexorably, against those who sought to destroy civilization.

Known for her humanitarian and charitable efforts, First Lady Eleanor Roosevelt helped spread Christmas cheer as she assisted the Salvation Army in distributing food baskets to the needy. (Library of Congress)

On this Christmas day, we cannot yet say when our victory will come. Our enemies still fight fanatically. They still have reserves of men and military power. But, they themselves know that they and their evil works are doomed. We may hasten the day of their doom if we here at home continue to do our full share.

And we pray that that day may come soon. We pray that until then, God will protect our gallant men and women in the uniforms of the United Nations—that He will receive into His infinite grace those who make their supreme sacrifice in the cause of righteousness, in the cause of love of Him and His teachings.

We pray that with victory will come a new day of peace on earth in which all the Nations of the earth will join together for all time. That is the spirit of Christmas, the holy day. May that spirit live and grow throughout the world in all the years to come.

(Franklin D. Roosevelt, "Address to the Nation," December 24, 1944.)

1945

Charting a Course for the Future

HARRY S. TRUMAN

HISTORICAL NOTE: Harry S. Truman had been Vice President for just eighty-three days before he was thrust into the presidency following the unexpected death of President Roosevelt on April 12, 1945. He recalled, "I felt like the moon, the stars, and all the planets had fallen on me." It would prove to be a pivotal time in the nation's history. In this address at the lighting of the National Christmas Tree later that same year, President Truman spoke to a nation at peace after four wartime Christmases. But the anticipated "long peace" was not to be. In President Truman's Christmas message one year later, he reported, "I am sorry to say all is not in harmony in the world today. We have found that it is easier for men to die together on the field of battle than it is for them to live together at home in peace." By 1952, the United States was embroiled in an undeclared war with North Korea.

A large crowd gathered on the grounds of the White House in 1945 for the lighting of the National Community Christmas Tree, with the South Portico in the background.
(Harry S. Truman Library and Museum)

This is the Christmas that a war-weary world has prayed for through long and awful years. With peace come joy and gladness. The gloom of the war years fades as once more we light the National Community Christmas Tree. We meet in the spirit of the first Christmas, when the midnight choir sang the hymn of joy: "Glory to God in the highest, and on earth peace, good will toward men."

Let us not forget that the coming of the Saviour brought a time of long peace to the Roman World. It is, therefore, fitting for us to remember that the spirit of

Christmas is the spirit of peace, of love, of charity to all men. From the manger of Bethlehem came a new appeal to the minds and hearts of men: "A new commandment I give unto you, that ye love one another."

In love, which is the very essence of the message of the Prince of Peace, the world would find a solution for all its ills. I do not believe there is one problem in this country or in the world today which could not be settled if approached through the teaching of the Sermon on the Mount. The poets' dream, the lesson of priest and patriarch and the prophets' vision of a new heaven and a new earth, all are summed up in the message delivered in the Judean hills beside the Sea of Galilee. Would that the world would accept that message in this time of its greatest need!

This is a solemn hour. In the stillness of the Eve of the Nativity when the hopes of mankind hang on the peace that was offered to the world nineteen centuries ago, it

In 1952, during the last year of the Truman administration, President Truman's message at the lighting of National Christmas Tree included a prayer "for all our service men and women wherever they are." He added, "Let us also pray for our enemies. Let us pray that the spirit of God shall enter their lives and prevail in their lands. Let us pray for a fulfillment of the brotherhood of man." That year, the Communist army in Korea announced a temporary ceasefire on Christmas morning to allow Allied troops to celebrate.

is but natural, while we survey our destiny, that we give thought also to our past—to some of the things which have gone into the making of our Nation.

You will remember that Saint Paul, the Apostle of the Gentiles, and his companions, suffering shipwreck, "cast four anchors out of the stern and wished for the day." Happily for us, whenever the American Ship of State has been storm-tossed we have always had an anchor to the windward.

We are met on the South Lawn of the White House. The setting is a reminder of Saint Paul's four anchors. To one side is the massive pile of the Washington Monument—fit symbol of our first anchor. On the opposite end of Potomac Park is the memorial to another of the anchors which we see when we look astern of the Ship of State—Abraham Lincoln, who preserved the Union that Washington wrought.

Between them is the memorial to Thomas Jefferson, the anchor of democracy. On the other side of the White House, in bronze, rides Andrew Jackson—fourth of our anchors—the pedestal of his monument bearing his immortal words: "Our Federal Union—it must be preserved."

President Truman delivers Christmas presents to family members. The President's family celebrated with gifts under the tree and singing carols around the piano. (Harry S. Truman Library and Museum)

It is well in this solemn hour that we bow to Washington, Jefferson, Jackson, and Lincoln as we face our destiny with its hopes and fears—its burdens and its responsibilities. Out of the past we shall gather wisdom and inspiration to chart our future course.

With our enemies vanquished we must gird ourselves for the work that lies ahead. Peace has its victories no less hard won than success at arms. We must not fail or falter. We must strive without ceasing to make real the prophecy of Isaiah: "They shall beat their swords into plowshares and their spears into pruning-hooks: nation shall not lift up sword against nation, neither shall they learn war any more."

In this day, whether it be far or near, the Kingdoms of this world shall become indeed the Kingdom of God and He will reign forever and ever, Lord of Lords and King of Kings. With that message I wish my countrymen a Merry Christmas and joyous days in the New Year.

(Harry S. Truman, "Address at the Lighting of the National Community Christmas Tree on the White House Grounds," December 24, 1945.)

1953
The Cold War
DWIGHT D. EISENHOWER

HISTORICAL NOTE: Following the signing of the Korean Armistice Agreement on July 27, 1953, America was no longer involved in armed conflict, but the tensions between Russia and the United States were evident in his first Christmas greeting to the nation. President Eisenhower, who had led the forces in Europe to victory during World War II, would continue to focus on maintaining world peace throughout his presidency.

My Fellow Americans—here in Washington, in your homes across the Nation and abroad—and in our country's service around the world:

This evening's ceremony, here at the White House,

is one of many thousands in America's traditional celebration of the birth, almost 2,000 years ago, of the Prince of Peace.

For us, this Christmas is truly a season of good will—and our first peaceful one since 1949. Our national and individual blessings are manifold. Our hopes are bright even though the world still stands divided in two antagonistic parts.

More precisely than in any other way, prayer places freedom and communism in opposition, one to the other. The Communist can find no reserve of strength in prayer because his doctrine of materialism and statism denies the dignity of man and consequently the existence of God. But in America, George Washington long ago rejected exclusive dependence upon mere materialistic values. In the bitter and critical winter at Valley Forge, when the cause of liberty was so near defeat, his recourse was sincere and earnest prayer. From it he received new hope and new strength of purpose out of which grew the freedom in which we celebrate this Christmas season.

As religious faith is the foundation of free government, so is prayer an indispensable part of that faith.

Tonight, richly endowed in the good things of the earth, in the fellowship of our neighbors and the love of our families, would it not be fitting for each of us to speak in prayer to the Father of all men and women on this earth, of whatever nation, and of every race and creed—to ask that He help us—and teach us—and strengthen us—and receive our thanks.

Should we not pray that He help us? Help us to remember that the founders of this, our country, came first to these shores in search of freedom—freedom of man

President Eisenhower was a talented artist and often painted for relaxation. His artwork included portraits of former presidents George Washington and Abraham Lincoln, as well as many family and friends. He also painted beautiful landscapes and still life images. During President Eisenhower's eight Christmases in the White House, six of his paintings were reproduced as gift prints and presented to his staff for Christmas.

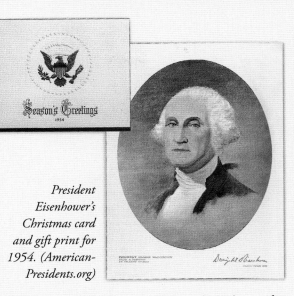

President Eisenhower's Christmas card and gift print for 1954. (American-Presidents.org)

to walk in dignity; to live without fear; beyond the yoke of tyranny; ever to progress. Help us to cherish freedom, for each of us and for all nations.

Might we not pray that He teach us? Teach us to shun the counsel of defeat and of despair, of self-pride and self-deceit. Teach us, and teach our leaders, to seek to understand the problems and the needs of all our people. Teach us how those problems may reach solution in wisdom and how best those needs may be met. But teach us, also,

The Eisenhower family steps from the north entrance of the White House bearing holiday gifts.
(National Archives)

that where there may be special problems, there can be no special rights; and though there may be special needs, there can be no special privileges. Teach us to require of all those who seek to lead us, these things: integrity of purpose; the upright mind, selfless sacrifice, and the courage of the just. Teach us trust and hope and self-dependence. Teach us the security of faith.

And may we pray that He strengthen us. Strengthen us in understanding ourselves and others—in our homes, in our country, and in our world. Strengthen our concern for brotherhood. Strengthen our conviction that whatever we, as Americans, would bring to pass in the world must first come to pass in the heart of America. Strengthen our efforts to forge abroad those links of friendship which must one day encircle the world, if its people are to survive and live in peace.

Lastly, should we not pray that He receive our thanks? For certainly we are grateful for all the good we find about us; for the opportunity given us to use our strength and our faith to meet the problems of this hour. And on this Christmas Eve, all hearts in America are filled with special thanks to God that the blood of those we love no longer spills on battlefields abroad. May He receive the thanks of each of us for this, His greatest bounty—and our supplication that peace on earth may live with us, always.

(Dwight D. Eisenhower, "Remarks upon Lighting the National Community Christmas Tree," December 24, 1953.)

1962

"The Most Sacred and Hopeful Day"
JOHN F. KENNEDY

HISTORICAL NOTE: With the Cuban Missile Crisis occurring just two months prior to this address, President Kennedy spoke of peace in this Christmas message to the American people. He expressed hope for peace after "a year of peril when the peace [had] been sorely threatened, [but] a year when peril was faced and when reason ruled." Because of this, he said, "We may talk, at this Christmas, just a little bit more confidently of peace on earth, good will to men." Tragically, this would be the last Christmas of President Kennedy's short life. He was assassinated on November 22, 1963.

With the lighting of this tree, which is an old ceremony in Washington and one which has been among the most important responsibilities of a good many Presidents of the United States, we initiate, in a formal way, the Christmas Season.

We mark the festival of Christmas which is the most sacred and hopeful day in our civilization. For nearly 2,000 years the message of Christmas, the message of peace and good will towards all men, has been the guiding star of our endeavors. This morning I had a meeting at the White House which included some of our repre-

sentatives from far-off countries in Africa and Asia. They were returning to their posts for the Christmas holidays. Talking with them afterwards, I was struck by the fact that in the far-off continents Moslems, Hindus, Buddhists, as well as Christians, pause from their labors on the 25th day of December to celebrate the birthday of the Prince of Peace. There could be no more striking proof that Christmas is truly the universal holiday of all men. It is the day when all of us dedicate our thoughts to others; when all are reminded that mercy and compassion are the enduring virtues; when all show, by small deeds and large and by acts, that

Test lighting the National Christmas Tree on the Ellipse in President's Park, December 15, 1962. (John F. Kennedy Presidential Library)

President John F. Kennedy and First Lady Jacqueline Kennedy stand in front of the 1961 Christmas tree in the Blue Room. (John F. Kennedy Presidential Library)

it is more blessed to give than to receive.

It is the day when we remind ourselves that man can and must live in peace with his neighbors and that it is the peacemakers who are truly blessed. In this year of 1962 we greet each other at Christmas with some special sense of the blessings of peace. This has been a year of peril when the peace has been sorely threatened. But it has been a year when peril was faced and when reason ruled. As a result, we may talk, at this Christmas, just a little bit more confidently of peace on earth, good will to men. As a result, the hopes of the American people are perhaps a little higher. We have much yet to do. We still need to ask that God bless everyone. But yet I think we can enter this season of good will with more than usual joy in our hearts.

And I think all of us extend a special word of gratitude and appreciation to those who serve the United States abroad; to the one million men in uniform who will celebrate this Christmas away from their homes; to those hundreds of young men and women and some older men and women who serve in far-off countries in our Peace Corps; to the members of the Foreign Service; to those who work in the various information services, AID agencies, and others who work for us abroad who will celebrate

President Kennedy hanging Christmas stockings at the family home in Palm Beach, Florida, which was nicknamed the "Winter White House." (John F. Kennedy Presidential Library)

this December 25th thousands of miles from us at sea, on land, and in the air, but with us. It is to them that we offer the best of Christmases and to all of you I send my very best wishes for a blessed and happy Christmas and a peaceful and prosperous New Year.

Thank you.

This [indicating the electric switch] was first pressed by President Coolidge in 1923 and succeedingly by President Hoover, Vice President Curtis, by President Franklin Roosevelt on many occasions, by President Harry Truman, by President Eisenhower, by Vice President Johnson. I am delighted to be in that illustrious company and we therefore light the tree.

(John F. Kennedy, "Remarks at the Pageant of Peace Ceremonies," December 17, 1962.)

1962 was the only year that President Kennedy participated in the lighting of the National Christmas Tree. In 1961, the President's first year in office, his 73-year-old father, Joseph F. Kennedy, suffered a stroke the day before the ceremony. The First Family flew to Palm Beach, Florida, to be at his side, and Vice President Lyndon B. Johnson attended the ceremony (renamed "Pageant of Peace" in 1954) in the President's place.

1963

"A Great National Sorrow"
LYNDON B. JOHNSON

HISTORICAL NOTE: Following the assassination of President Kennedy, a month of official mourning was declared across the United States. The lighting of the National Christmas Tree was postponed from December 18 to December 22. To mark the end of thirty days of mourning, a candlelight memorial service was held at the Lincoln Memorial just prior to the tree-lighting ceremony. President Johnson spoke of the slain President in his remarks and expressed the wish that the "nation would not lose the closeness and the sense of sharing and the spirit of mercy and compassion, which these last few days have brought to us all."

Tonight we come to the end of the season of great national sorrow, and to the beginning of the season of great, eternal joy. We mourn our great

President, John F. Kennedy, but he would have us go on. While our spirits cannot be light, our hearts need not be heavy.

We were taught by Him whose birth we commemorate that after death there is life. We can believe, and we do believe, that from the death of our national leader will come a rebirth of the finest qualities of our national life.

View of the North Portico of the White House, draped in black mourning crepe during the 1963 Christmas season, following the death of President Kennedy on November 22, 1963. (John F. Kennedy Presidential Library)

On this same occasion thirty years ago, at the close of another troubled year in our Nation's history, a great President, Franklin D. Roosevelt, said to his countrymen, "To more and more of us the words 'Thou shalt love thy neighbor as thyself' have taken on a meaning that is showing itself and proving itself in our purposes and in our daily lives."

I believe that this is no less true for all of us in all of our regions of our land today.

There is a turning away from things which are false and things which are small, and things which are shallow.

There is a turning toward those things which are true, those things which are profound, and those things which are eternal. We can, we do, live tonight in new hope and new

The day after issuing a challenge to the American public to "devote time to sharing with others," President Johnson held an impromptu party at the White House for all members of Congress and their spouses. With only five hours to plan and prepare for an event involving two hundred guests, the White House staff enlisted help from other divisions of the government to replace the black mourning crepe that had draped doorways and fixtures with fresh evergreen boughs and flowers, holly, wreaths, and a fully-decorated twelve-foot Christmas tree.

confidence and new faith in ourselves and in what we can do together through the future.

Our need for such faith was never greater, for we are the heirs of a great trust. In these last two hundred years we have guided the building of our Nation and our society by those principles and precepts brought to earth nearly 2,000 years ago on that first Christmas.

We have our faults and we have our failings, as any mortal society must. But when sorrow befell us, we learned anew how great is the trust and how close is the kinship that mankind feels for us, and most of all, that we feel for each other. We must remember, and we must never forget, that the hopes and the fears of all the years rest with us, as with no other people in all history. We shall keep that trust working, as always we have worked, for peace on earth and good will among men.

On this occasion a year ago, our beloved President John F. Kennedy reminded us that Christmas is the day when all of us dedicate our thoughts to others, when we are

The Johnson family on Christmas Eve 1968 in the Yellow Oval room at the White House.
(LBJ Library)

all reminded that mercy and compassion are the really enduring virtues, when all of us show, by small deeds and by large, that it is more blessed to give than to receive.

So in that spirit tonight, let me express to you as your President the one wish that I have as we gather here. It is a wish that we not lose the closeness and the sense of sharing, and the spirit of mercy and compassion which these last few days have brought for us all.

Between tonight and Christmas Eve, let each American family, whatever their station, whatever their religion, whatever their race or their region—let each American family devote time to sharing with others something of themselves; yes, something of their very own. Let us, if we can do no more, lend a hand and share an hour, and say a prayer—and find some way with which to make this Christmas a prouder memory for what we gave instead of what we receive.

And now here, as we have done so many years, we turn on, in your Capital City, the lights of our National Christmas Tree, and we say that we hope that the world will not narrow into a neighborhood before it has broadened into a brotherhood.

(Lyndon B. Johnson, "Remarks at the Lighting of the Nation's Christmas Tree," December 22, 1963.)

A painting of the Blue Room Christmas tree. Given as a gift print by President and Mrs. Johnson. (White House)

1973

"Problems of Peace"
RICHARD M. NIXON

HISTORICAL NOTE: 1973 marked the fiftieth anniversary of the lighting of the National Christmas Tree and the first Christmas in twelve years in which U.S. troops were not committed in military conflict in Vietnam. But with a looming energy crisis and talk of impeachment due to charges stemming from the Watergate scandal, it was a turbulent time in American history. Although the President spoke of the coming new year as a time for overcoming challenges, this would his last Christmas greeting to the nation before resigning from office on August 8, 1974.

I think one of the greatest privileges that a President of the United States has is to light the Christmas tree, the Nation's Christmas tree, because it belongs to all the Nation, here in the Nation's Capital.

This year, as the Secretary [Rogers C. B. Morton, Secretary of the Interior] has already indicated, the tree is different. This year, Christmas will be different in terms of lights, perhaps, all across America. Instead of having many lights on the tree, as you will see over there in a few moments, there will be only one on it, the star at the top, and the other lights you see will simply be the glitter from the ground lights which are around the tree.

The Nixon family at Christmastime in the White House. (Nixon Presidential Library and Museum)

And in a way, I suppose one could say with only one light on the tree, this will be a very dreary Christmas, but we know that isn't true, because the spirit of Christmas is not measured by the number of lights on a tree. The spirit of Christmas is measured by the love that each of us has in his heart for his family, for his friends, for his fellow Americans, and for people all over the world. And this year, while we have a problem, a problem the Secretary has alluded to, the problem of energy, I think that what we can all be thankful for is that it is a problem of peace and not a problem of war. That is what Americans can be thankful for.

This year we will drive a little slower. This year the thermostats will be a little lower. This year every American perhaps will sacrifice a little, but no one will suffer. But we will do it for a great goal, the goal, first, of seeing to it that in a year when our energy supplies are not as high as we need, we can prepare for the future, and also a year in which America will make a great stride forward toward a new, great goal, and that is, by the year 1980 this Nation, which will celebrate its 200th anniversary of independence in 1976—by 1980 will celebrate Project Independence, when we are independent of any other country in the world where our energy supply is concerned. That we can do.

Pat Nixon displays an ornament from one of the White House Christmas trees. She began some of the more popular holiday traditions such as the annual gingerbread house and candlelight tours. (Richard Nixon Foundation)

As we consider these problems of peace, I think also we must be thankful, as the Secretary has already indicated, for the fact that this is the first Christmas in twelve years that a President has stood here at a time when America was at peace with every nation in the world.

It is the first Christmas in eight years when no American prisoner of war is away from home at Christmas. And to all of these young people, and particularly to our very distinguished young people who participated in this program, it is also a Christmas for the first time in twenty years when no young American is being drafted for the armed services. That is what peace means to America.

It would be well, of course, for us to stand simply on that achievement, but we know that there will always be threats to the peace of the world, and that is where we come in, and where each American comes in, looking to the future. Because as we look at the chances not just of getting peace, which we have now achieved, but of keeping peace, which we have not been able to do for a full generation, for a century, then what happens in America will decide it, whether America has the strength not just of its arms but more, of its spirit to provide the leadership that the world needs to keep the trouble spots in the world from blowing up into war and to build that permanent structure of peace that we all want.

It is that to which we dedicate ourselves as we light the Nation's Christmas tree tonight. Let the year 1974 be one in which we make great progress toward the goal of a lasting peace, peace not only for America but for all nations, peace between peoples who have different forms of government, but who nevertheless can be friends.

A moment ago when the flowers were presented to Mrs. Nixon by Tyna [Tyna A.

The traditional nativity scene was eliminated from the 1973 Pageant of Peace festival after a U.S. Court of Appeals ruled that it violated the First Amendment and represented "excessive entanglement" of the government in religion. A year earlier, the conventional star that had topped the National Christmas Tree was replaced with a snowflake design due to legal action. Today a private organization hosts a nativity display near the Pageant of Peace exhibit on the Ellipse.

Lee of the Camp Fire Girls of America], I remembered an occasion in 1959 when a little girl presented flowers to her in the Ural Mountains in Russia. We were driving through the mountains, and a group of schoolchildren stopped the cavalcade for a few moments and they presented flowers to Mrs. Nixon. And when they did so in this year 1959, when the Cold War was still going on, they shouted out "Friendship, friendship" in English. When we got back into the car, our guide, Mr. Zhukov, said to me that the first word that a Russian child who learns English and studies English in a Russian school learns is the word "friendship." That is the first English word the Russian child learns.

Now, I do not mean to suggest by that that because a Russian child is taught, when he first studies English, the word "friendship" that it is inevitable that the Russian people and the American people are not going to have differences as far as their governments are concerned, but I do know this: We have had the great privilege, Mrs. Nixon and I, of traveling to most of the nations of the world, to the nations of Africa, to the nations of Asia, to China, to Russia, and I can tell you that the people of the world want peace, the people of the world want friendship, and every American, I know, wants his country and his Government to take the lead in building a world of peace.

As this Christmas season begins, let us just remember we do have some problems which we will overcome, but they are the problems of peace. And we also have a great challenge, the challenge of helping to build a structure of peace that all the three billion people in this world can enjoy. What a wonderful achievement that can be.

There are times, of course, when we tire of the challenge. There are times when we would not like to accept that position of leadership, but let us remember that unless America, at this time in history, accepts the responsibility to lead for peace, we may not have it in the world.

Pat and Richard Nixon in front of the White House. (Richard Nixon Foundation)

I think we can meet the challenge. I am sure we will. And on this particular day, in this year 1973, as we look at the beginning of the year 1974, let us so conduct ourselves as a people, let us so conduct ourselves as a nation in our leadership toward peace that in the years to come, people, not only in America but all over the world, will look back at what we have done, will look back and say "God bless America."

Thank you.

(Richard M. Nixon, "Remarks at the Lighting of the Nation's Christmas Tree," December 14, 1973.)

1974
Hope for a Brighter Year Ahead
GERALD FORD

HISTORICAL NOTE: *Gerald Ford had been President for just four months prior to delivering his first official Christmas message to a nation still reeling from the turmoil of Watergate, a continuing energy crisis, and worsening economic conditions. Despite his con-*

troversial decision to pardon Richard Nixon for any crimes he may have committed during his term of office, President Ford dispensed with protocol and invited members of Congress from both sides of the aisle to a White House gala following the lighting of the National Christmas Tree. Addressing his guests, President Ford drew a comparison between himself and the White House tree. "That tree and I have a lot in common," he said. "Neither one of us expected to be in the White House a few months ago."

Obviously, I am very delighted to participate in this celebration tonight, to light and to share with you the Nation's Christmas tree.

As a former National Park Service ranger a good many years ago, I have been and am concerned with conservation. I am pleased to know, of course, that this tree has a heritage from Colorado but was transplanted here from the great State of Pennsylvania. But this tree will be the National Community Christmas Tree and will be so for many, many years to come.

As a President vitally concerned with the saving of energy, I also want you to know that the electricity consumed, as the Secretary of Interior [Rogers C. B. Morton] has said, is a considerable reduction of what has been used in years past. And that is the way it should be, and that is the way that it must be.

President Gerald Ford, First Lady Betty Ford, and daughter Susan Ford at a White House Christmas party. (Library of Congress)

The glow of Christmas, however, should come from a power source which we will never run short of, our abiding faith and our love of God.

The true spirit of this season can best be seen in our faces. The children here tonight, like millions of children around the world, reflect the wonder and the

In 1975, the National Christmas Tree was patriotically decorated with red, white, and blue ornaments and topped with a specially designed four-foot replica of the Liberty Bell to commemorate the upcoming Bicentennial year. The tree was circled by thirteen smaller trees representing the original thirteen colonies. In his Christmas greeting to the nation, President Ford said, "In our two hundred years, we Americans have always honored the spiritual testament of 2,000 years ago. We embrace the spirit of the Prince of Peace so that we might find peace in our own hearts and in our own land, and hopefully in the world as well."

excitement of anticipation. Those of us who are older look forward to the warmth of reunions with families and with friends.

Traditions, treasured memories, shared hopes—these are the ties that bind families together and nations together. The tree before us is a part of our national tradition, and as such, it has seen both triumphs and tragedies.

Christmas and the New Year have always been a time to reflect on the past and then look ahead to the future. I firmly believe that 1975 will be a brighter year for all America, but it must also be a brighter year for the world around us, the entire globe, if we as a nation are to prosper.

And so, I would like to share with you my personal list of Christmas wishes. At the top of my list are peace, economic well-being for all, and a caring climate that will permit everyone to achieve the fullest potential of their human gifts. And I wish this

Nation a strong future out of a very proud past. And I wish every one of us the realization of love and belonging.

Billions of words over the years have been written, have been sung, have been spoken about the true meaning of Christmas. None have ever said it more eloquently than "on earth peace, good will toward men." And that is my final Christmas wish for all of us.

Thank you very kindly.

(Gerald R. Ford, "Remarks for Christmas Tree Lighting Ceremony," December 17, 1974.)

First Lady Betty Ford and daughter Susan Ford make holiday ornaments in the White House Solarium. (White House)

1979

"Come Home Safe"
JIMMY CARTER

HISTORICAL NOTE: On November 4, 1979, the U.S. Embassy in Iran was unexpectedly attacked and fifty Americans were taken hostage. President Carter's message at the lighting of the National Christmas Tree that year reflected the somber mood of the country and concern for the plight of the hostages. To the surprise of the audience, President Carter announced that only the star at the top of the main tree and the lights on the fifty smaller Christmas trees (which traditionally represented each of the fifty states) would be lit—one for each of the hostages. The rest of the lights, he informed the crowd, would be turned on when the hostages returned home. No one knew then that another Christmas would come and go before the hostages were released.

Christmas means a lot of things. It means love. It means warmth. It means friendship. It means family. It means joy. It means light. But everyone this Christmas will not be experiencing those deep feelings. At this moment there are fifty Americans who don't have freedom, who don't have joy, and who don't have warmth, who don't have their families with them. And there are fifty American families in this Nation who also will not experience all the joys and the light and the happiness of Christmas.

I think it would be appropriate for all those in this audience and for all those listening to my voice or watching on television to pause just for a few seconds in a silent prayer that American hostages will come home safe and come home soon—if you'd please join me just for a moment.

[Pause for silent prayer.]

Thank you very much.

Nineteen seventy-nine has not been a bad year. Many good things have happened to us individually and have also happened to our Nation. Not far from here, on the north side of the White House, we saw a remarkable ceremony, headed by a Jew, the leader of Israel, a Moslem, the President of Egypt, and myself, a Christian, the President of our country, signing a treaty of peace. This peace treaty was a historic development, and it was compatible with the commitment that we feel so deeply in the religious season now upon us.

Our Nation also opened up its arms of understanding,

President Jimmy Carter lights the Menorah in front of the White House with Rabbi Abraham Shemto. (Jimmy Carter Library and Museum)

diplomatic relationships, and friendship—our Nation, the strongest on Earth, and China, the most populous nation on Earth. The establishment of new friendships is part of the Christmas Season.

I went to Vienna and met with President Brezhnev. And he and I signed the SALT II treaty, which will help to limit and to reduce the spread of nuclear weapons, to bring about a better understanding between our two great countries, and to search for the kind of reduction of armaments that will lead, I think, to the realization of the true spirit of Christmas.

This fall we had a visit from a great spiritual leader, Pope John Paul II, who traveled throughout our country and who spoke in a quiet voice of understanding, of compassion, of love, of commitment, of morality, of ethics, of the unchanging things that are part of the spirit of Christmas. And I remember one thing in particular that he said on the White House lawn. He said, "Do not be afraid. Do not be afraid." And as you know, that's the same message that the angels brought to the shepherds near Bethlehem the night that our Savior was born: "Fear not. Be not afraid." Many of the problems in our world derive from fear, from a lack of confidence in ourselves and, particularly, a lack of confidence in what we can do, with God.

We hope we'll soon see peace in Zimbabwe-Rhodesia, a nation that has suffered much in the last few years. But we've also seen some needs for additional effort.

This is the Year of the Child, but it's possibly true that in Cambodia, or Kampuchea, the children will have suffered more in 1979 than in any other year in our lifetime—children so weak, so starved, that they don't even have the strength to cry. We've seen Vietnam refugees put to sea with very little hope of ever reaching land

First Lady Rosalynn Carter with the 1979 folk art ornaments designed by Tim Gunn.
(Jimmy Carter Library and Museum)

again. And our country has reached out its arms to help those starving children and those refugees adrift.

We've seen divisions among people because of religious beliefs. The recent events in Iran are an unfortunate example of that misguided application of belief in God. But I know that all Americans feel very deeply that the relationships between ourselves and the Moslem believers in the world of Islam is one of respect and care and brotherhood and good will and love.

So, we do have disappointments; we do have suffering; we do have divisions; we often have war. But in the midst of pain, we can still remember what Christmas is—a time of joy, a time of light, a time of warmth, a time of families, and a time of peace.

The unlit 1979 National Christmas Tree with the Washington Monument in the background. (Executive Office of the President of the United States)

In our great country we have an awful lot for which we can be thankful: the birth of our Savior, the initiation of religious holidays tomorrow night for the Jews of America, and a realization that in our Nation we do have freedom to worship or not worship as we please. So, let's remember our blessings, yes, but let's also remember the needs for us to be more fervent in our belief in God and especially in the sharing of our blessings with others.

Thank you very much. Merry Christmas to you all.

And now we'll go over—Amy and I

1979 was only the second time since World War II that the National Christmas Tree was not lit during the Christmas season. Although President Carter had hoped for an early release of the hostages, the following year the tree was lit for just 417 seconds, one second of light for each day the hostages had spent in captivity. On the day of Ronald Reagan's inauguration, January 20, 1981, word was received that the hostages had been released. For the first time, the National Christmas Tree was lit during the month of January.

and Rosalynn—and we'll light the lights that signify Christmas. Thank you very much. Is everybody ready?

I'm going to ask Amy to throw the switch. [At this point, Amy Carter threw the switch that lit the star on top of the National Community Christmas Tree and the lights on the fifty smaller trees, which traditionally represent the fifty states.]

I want to tell you what just happened. Around the periphery of this crowd, there are fifty small Christmas trees, one for each American hostage and on the top of the great Christmas tree is a star of hope. We will turn on the other lights on the tree when the American hostages come home. Merry Christmas, everybody.

(Jimmy Carter, "Christmas Pageant of Peace Remarks on Lighting the National Community Christmas Tree," December 13, 1979.)

1981

A Spirit of Solidarity

RONALD REAGAN

HISTORICAL NOTE: This 1981 Christmas address was given during President Reagan's first Christmas in the White House. It was a turbulent time in world politics. That year, the North Portico of the White House was adorned with a single candle flickering in a window to show solidarity with the Polish struggle. The citizens of Poland, who were under martial law at this time, also lit candles placed in their windows to show that the light of liberty still glowed in their hearts. When President Reagan spoke out in his address against the persecution of the Solidarity Movement and its leaders by the Soviet-backed government of Poland, few could have foreseen that this would be the beginning of the end for the Communist Bloc and the Soviet Union.

Good evening.

At Christmas time, every home takes on a special beauty, a special warmth, and that's certainly true of the White House, where so many famous Americans have spent their Christmases over the years. This fine old home, the people's house, has seen so much, been so much a part of all our lives and history. It's been humbling and inspiring for Nancy and me to be spending our first Christmas in this place.

We've lived here as your tenants for almost a year now, and what a year it's been. As a people we've been through quite a lot—moments of joy, of tragedy, and of real achievement—moments that I believe have brought us all closer together. G. K. Chesterton once said that the world would never starve for wonders, but only for the want of wonder.

At this special time of year, we all renew our sense of wonder in recalling the story of the first Christmas in Bethlehem, nearly 2,000 years ago.

Some celebrate Christmas as the birthday of a great and good philosopher and teacher. Others of us believe in the

President Reagan and Nancy Reagan official photo with Christmas tree in the Blue Room, December 1981. (Ronald Reagan Presidential Library)

divinity of the child born in Bethlehem, that he was and is the promised Prince of Peace. Yes, we've questioned why he who could perform miracles chose to come among us as a helpless babe, but maybe that was his first miracle, his first great lesson that we should learn to care for one another.

Tonight, in millions of American homes, the glow of the Christmas tree is a reflection of the love Jesus taught us. Like the shepherds and wise men of that first

Nancy Reagan accepts the 1983 White House Christmas tree at the North Portico.
(Ronald Reagan Presidential Library)

Christmas, we Americans have always tried to follow a higher light, a star, if you will. At lonely campfire vigils along the frontier, in the darkest days of the Great Depression, through war and peace, the twin beacons of faith and freedom have brightened the American sky. At times our footsteps may have faltered, but trusting in God's help, we've never lost our way.

Just across the way from the White House stand the two great emblems of the holiday season: a Menorah, symbolizing the Jewish festival of Hanukkah, and the National Christmas Tree, a beautiful, towering blue spruce from Pennsylvania. Like the National Christmas Tree, our country is a living, growing thing planted in rich American soil. Only our devoted care can bring it to full flower. So, let this holiday season be for us a time of rededication.

Even as we rejoice, however, let us remember that for some Americans, this will not be as happy a Christmas as it should be. I know a little of what they feel. I remember one Christmas Eve during the Great Depression, my father opening what he thought was a Christmas greeting. It was a notice that he no longer had a job.

Over the past year, we've begun the long, hard work of economic recovery. Our goal is an America in which every citizen who needs and wants a job can get a job. Our program for recovery has only been in place for twelve weeks now, but it is beginning to work. With your help and prayers, it will succeed. We're winning the battle against inflation, runaway government spending, and taxation, and that victory will mean more economic growth, more jobs, and more opportunity for all Americans.

A few months before he took up residence in this house, one of my predecessors, John Kennedy, tried to sum up the temper of the times with a quote from an author

According to the White House Historical Association, President Benjamin Harrison, in 1889, was the first president to install an indoor Christmas tree in the White House. It was decorated with ornaments and candles. In 1929, First Lady Lou Henry Hoover oversaw what would become an annual tradition of decorating the indoor White House tree, a duty assumed by each First Lady since. In 1981, President Ronald Reagan began another custom by authorizing the first official White House Christmas tree ornament, copies of which were then made available for purchase.

closely tied to Christmas, Charles Dickens. We were living, he said, in the best of times and the worst of times. Well, in some ways that's even more true today. The world is full of peril, as well as promise. Too many of its people, even now, live in the shadow of want and tyranny.

As I speak to you tonight, the fate of a proud and ancient nation hangs in the balance. For a thousand years, Christmas has been celebrated in Poland, a land of deep religious faith, but this Christmas brings little joy to the courageous Polish people. They have been betrayed by their own government.

The men who rule them and their totalitarian allies fear the very freedom that the Polish people cherish. They have answered the stirrings of liberty with brute force, killings, mass arrests, and the setting up of concentration camps. Lech Walesa and other Solidarity leaders are imprisoned, their fate unknown. Factories, mines, universities, and homes have been assaulted.

The Polish government has trampled underfoot solemn commitments to the UN Charter and the Helsinki accords. It has even broken the Gdansk agreement of August 1980, by which the Polish government recognized the basic right of its people to form free trade unions and to strike.

The tragic events now occurring in Poland, almost two years to the day after the Soviet invasion of Afghanistan, have been precipitated by public and secret pressure from the Soviet Union. It is no coincidence that Soviet Marshal Kulikov, chief of the Warsaw Pact forces, and other senior Red Army officers were in Poland while these outrages were being initiated. And it is no coincidence that the martial law proclamations imposed in December by the Polish government were being printed in the Soviet Union in September.

White House candlelight vigil for Poland. (Ronald Reagan Presidential Library)

The target of this depression [repression] is the Solidarity Movement, but in attacking Solidarity its enemies attack an entire people. Ten million of Poland's thirty-six million citizens are members of Solidarity. Taken together with their families, they account for the overwhelming majority of the Polish nation. By persecuting Solidarity the Polish government wages war against its own people.

I urge the Polish government and its allies to consider the consequences of their actions. How can they possibly justify using naked force to crush a people who ask for nothing more than the right to lead their own lives in freedom and dignity? Brute force may intimidate, but it cannot form the basis of an enduring society, and the ailing Polish economy cannot be rebuilt with terror tactics.

Poland needs cooperation between its government and its people, not military oppression. If the Polish government will honor the commitments it has made to human rights in documents like the Gdansk agreement, we in America will gladly do our share to help the shattered Polish economy, just as we helped the countries of Europe after both World Wars.

The 1981 National Christmas Tree. (White House)

It's ironic that we offered, and Poland expressed interest in accepting, our help after World War II. The Soviet Union intervened then and refused to allow such help to Poland. But if the forces of tyranny in Poland, and those who incite them from without, do not relent, they should prepare themselves for serious consequences. Already, throughout the free world, citizens have publicly demonstrated their support for the Polish people. Our government, and those of our allies, have expressed moral revulsion at the police state tactics of Poland's oppressors. The Church has also spoken out, in spite of threats and intimidation. But our reaction cannot stop there.

I want emphatically to state tonight that if the outrages in Poland do not cease, we cannot and will not conduct "business as usual" with the perpetrators and those who aid and abet them. Make no mistake, their crime will cost them dearly in their future dealings with America and free peoples everywhere. I do not make this statement lightly or without serious reflection.

We have been measured and deliberate in our reaction to the tragic events in Poland. We have not acted in haste, and the steps I will outline tonight and others we may take in the days ahead are firm, just, and reasonable.

In order to aid the suffering Polish people during this critical period, we will continue the shipment of food through private humanitarian channels, but only so long as we know that the Polish people themselves receive the food. The neighboring country of Austria has opened her doors to refugees from Poland. I have therefore directed that American assistance, including supplies of basic foodstuffs, be offered to aid the Austrians in providing for these refugees.

But to underscore our fundamental opposition to the repressive actions taken by the Polish government against its own people, the administration has suspended all government-sponsored shipments of agricultural and dairy products to the Polish government. This suspension will remain in force until absolute assurances are received that distribution of these products is monitored and guaranteed by independent agencies. We must be sure that every bit of food provided by America goes to the Polish people, not to their oppressors.

The United States is taking immediate action to suspend major elements of our economic relationships with the Polish government. We have halted the renewal of the Export-Import Bank's line of export credit insurance to the Polish government. We will suspend Polish civil aviation privileges in the United States. We are suspending the right of Poland's fishing fleet to operate in American waters. And we're proposing to our allies the further restriction of high technology exports to Poland.

These actions are not directed against the Polish people. They are a warning to the government of Poland that free men cannot and will not stand idly by in the face of brutal repression. To underscore this point, I've written a letter to General Jaruzelski, head of the Polish government. In it, I outlined the steps we're taking and warned of the serious consequences if the Polish government continues to use violence against its populace. I've urged him to free those in arbitrary detention, to lift martial law, and to restore the internationally recognized rights of the Polish people to free speech and association.

The Soviet Union, through its threats and pressures, deserves a major share of blame for the developments in Poland. So, I have also sent a letter to President Brezhnev urging him to permit the restoration of basic human rights in Poland provided for in the Helsinki Final Act. In it, I informed him that if this repression continues, the United States will have no choice but to take further concrete political and economic measures affecting our relationship.

When nineteenth-century Polish patriots rose against foreign oppressors, their rallying cry was, "For our freedom and yours." Well, that motto still rings true in our time. There is a spirit of solidarity abroad in the world tonight that no physical force

President Ronald Reagan and First Lady Nancy Reagan decorating the family
Christmas tree in the White House. (White House Historical Association)

can crush. It crosses national boundaries and enters into the hearts of men and women everywhere. In factories, farms, and schools, in cities and towns around the globe, we the people of the free world stand as one with our Polish brothers and sisters. Their cause is ours, and our prayers and hopes go out to them this Christmas.

Yesterday, I met in this very room with Romuald Spasowski, the distinguished former Polish ambassador who has sought asylum in our country in protest of the suppression of his native land. He told me that one of the ways the Polish people have demonstrated their solidarity in the face of martial law is by placing lighted candles in their windows to show that the light of liberty still glows in their hearts.

Ambassador Spasowski requested that on Christmas Eve a lighted candle will burn

First Lady Nancy Reagan assists in trimming the White House Christmas tree. (Ronald Reagan Presidential Library)

in the White House window as a small but certain beacon of our solidarity with the Polish people. I urge all of you to do the same tomorrow night, on Christmas Eve, as a personal statement of your commitment to the steps we're taking to support the brave people of Poland in their time of troubles.

Once, earlier in this century, an evil influence threatened that the lights were going out all over the world. Let the light of millions of candles in American homes give notice that the light of freedom is not going to be extinguished. We are blessed with a freedom and abundance denied to so many. Let those candles remind us that these blessings bring with them a solid obligation, an obligation to the God who guides us, an obligation to the heritage of liberty and dignity handed down to us by our forefathers and an obligation to the children of the world, whose future will be shaped by the way we live our lives today.

Christmas means so much because of one special child. But Christmas also reminds us that all children are special, that they are gifts from God, gifts beyond price that mean more than any presents money can buy. In their love and laughter, in our hopes for their future lies the true meaning of Christmas.

So, in a spirit of gratitude for what we've been able to achieve together over the past year and looking forward to all that we hope to achieve together in the years ahead, Nancy and I want to wish you all the best of holiday seasons. As Charles Dickens, whom I quoted a few moments ago, said so well in *A Christmas Carol*, "God bless us, every one."

Good night.

(Ronald Reagan, "Address to the Nation about Christmas and the Situation in Poland," December 23, 1981.)

1991

"The Bright Light of Liberty"
GEORGE H. W. BUSH

HISTORICAL NOTE: *Following the Persian Gulf War and the liberation of Kuwait the previous year, Christmas 1991 was notable due to the return of five Americans who had spent the prior Christmas chained and blindfolded as hostages in Lebanon. President George H. W. Bush invited the former hostages to light the National Christmas Tree, which had been decorated in patriotic red, white and blue lights.*

This is a very special night. And I look over my shoulder here at the very special guests, the brave men who are with us here tonight. And on behalf of our loving country I say, finally, to Terry Anderson, to Tom Sutherland, Joseph Cicippio, and Alann Steen and Jesse Turner, and the others not here: Welcome home.

Welcome home, to this, the most generous and proud and free Nation on the face of the Earth. It is more than just appropriate, it is almost miraculous that we can celebrate with these five the lighting of our Nation's Christmas tree. The idea is so moving because these men have come out of darkness into the bright light of liberty. And as you hear these remarkable men talk, you realize they were never lost in that darkness of sorrow, anguish, and despair. Even at the worst moments, they were guided by a stubborn spark that cruelty could not extinguish, the spark of the human spirit.

President and Mrs. Bush in front of the White House Christmas tree. (George Bush Presidential Library and Museum)

Their precious gift to us is to rekindle our Nation's belief in the light of faith and our belief in ourselves. And when Terry and Tom and Joseph and Alann and Jesse light our Nation's tree tonight, that act will be a reminder of what they and their companions, living and gone, have already done to light our Nation's soul.

There have been special guests at these ceremonies before. Even Winston Churchill helped to light the tree during World War II, but this Nation has never been honored by the presence of men whose spirit meant more to all of us. Your fortitude, your humor, and generosity tell us the true meaning of this season. And at this time of year

The painting for the 1991 White House Christmas card was created by impressionist artist Kamil Kubik, who had escaped Communist rule in his native Czechoslovakia in 1948. The painting was the first view of the family quarters at the White House to be featured on the annual White House Christmas card. Kubik described the experience as "a great honor." He explained, "During World War II, I escaped from the Communists and found refuge in the American army . . . the President, as Commander-in-Chief, is the Guardian Angel (of the civilized world). For me, to be able to do something for the President, I would drop everything at any time."

The Family Tree,
Upstairs at the White House

(White House Historical Association)

especially, these men remind us that the glitz and glamour of material things don't matter; the courage, the faith, and the love of these men embody, that they embody, are all we need to recognize what's really important.

The way they've returned to their families and to us proves they live by the challenge of that beautiful prayer of St. Francis, "Grant that I may not so much seek to be consoled as to console; to be understood as to understand; to be loved as to love.

Where there is despair, let us sow hope; where there is hatred, love; and where there is darkness, ever light."

When history remembers Christmas 1991, let it remember that tonight we gathered with men who show us that this is a season of spirit, not a celebration of plenty.

Let history remember that tonight we stood with these two heroes and asked for God's blessing on this world. And finally, in the words of the carol we'll sing in a few minutes, let history remember that at Christmas 1991, this Nation united to give thanks to God and to ask God for peace on earth, goodwill to all.

God bless these five men, this wonderful country, and now I'd like to ask them to join me as we light the Nation's Christmas tree.

(George H. W. Bush, "Remarks on Lighting the National Christmas Tree," December 12, 1991.)

President Bush reads Christmas stories to his grandchildren at Camp David, December 1991. (George Bush Presidential Library and Museum)

1999

The Dawn of a New Millennium
WILLIAM J. CLINTON

HISTORICAL NOTE: The country celebrated many "lasts" during the final Christmas season of the twentieth century, but most Americans focused on the year ahead as they awaited the dawn of a new millennium. On the heels of the political and legal turmoil of 1998 that had resulted in President Clinton's impeachment by the House of Representatives, his message to the nation in 1999 was one of peace and goodwill.

For over eighty-five years now, our country has gathered around our National Christmas Tree to celebrate the beginning of this wonderful season of peace and hope. I am honored once again to be part of a tradition I have come to look forward to every year.

For me, Christmas always starts now with the Pageant of Peace and the lighting of this beautiful Colorado spruce. And I am especially honored to be here to light the last tree of the twentieth century.

In this sacred season, it is time for all of us to renew our commitment to give of ourselves, to reach out to those who are less fortunate, to reach out to those who are different from us, to build the one America of our dreams. In this Pageant of Peace, we celebrate Christmas, also the season of Hanukkah and Kwanzaa and others, all joined by a simple and universal message, that we are to love our neighbors as ourselves.

This holiday season, we Americans have an awful lot to be thankful for: Our Nation is at peace, and all around the world we are privileged to make peace, from Bosnia to Northern Ireland to the Middle East, the land where a homeless child grew up to be the Prince of Peace.

President Bill Clinton and First Lady Hillary Clinton stand in front of the White House Christmas tree. (National Archives)

November 1, 2000, marked the two hundredth anniversary of the White House. When President John Adams moved into the unfinished building on November 1, 1800, he recorded, "I pray Heaven to bestow the best blessings on this house, and on all that shall hereafter inhabit it. May none but honest and wise men ever rule under this roof!" Those words are now engraved in the marble mantel of the State Dining Room.

Just today, in this season, I was proud to announce that after a long, long stalemate, the Israelis and the Syrians have agreed to meet again in just a few days to make their peace.

At the dawn of a new millennium, as we enjoy these wonderful performers and the timeless songs of all of our childhoods, let us rededicate ourselves to the true spirit of Christmas. As we light the National Christmas Tree, let us spread the light of peace and good will toward our family, our friends, our neighbors, and all those across the world, especially those who need it most.

Merry Christmas, happy new year, and God bless you.

(William J. Clinton, "Remarks on Lighting the National Christmas Tree," December 8, 1999.)

*Chef Mesnier's gingerbread White House in 1993 was titled the "House of Socks,"
and featured marzipan sculptures of the First Family's famous cat.
(White House Historical Association)*

2001
"We Will Not Forget"
GEORGE W. BUSH

HISTORICAL NOTE: Just three months after the September 11, 2001, attack by terrorists brought down the Twin Towers of the World Trade Center and inflicted heavy damage at the Pentagon, President George Bush stood behind protective glass and reminded the nation that even in "a time of testing," America would continue to celebrate the Christmas season as they had done in extraordinary times before. As noted by The Washington Post, *the lighting of the National Christmas Tree "was a sign of normalcy and tradition in a year that has been anything but normal and traditional."*

During this time of conflict and challenge, we once again celebrate the season of hope and the season of joy. We give thanks to our Nation and to our families and to our friends. . . .

In a moment, we will light the National Christmas Tree, a tradition Americans have been celebrating since 1923. The history of this event has included some memorable moments, including sixty years ago, less than three weeks after the attack on Pearl Harbor, when Prime Minister Winston Churchill made an appearance with President Franklin Roosevelt to light the tree.

Now once again, we celebrate Christmas in a time of testing, with American troops far from home. This season finds our country with losses to mourn and great tasks to complete. In all those tasks, it is worth recalling the words from a beautiful Christmas hymn. In the third verse of "O Holy Night," we sing, "His law is love, and His gospel is peace. Chains ye shall break, for the slave is our brother. And in His name all oppression shall cease."

"Thy face, Lord, do I seek: I believe that I shall see the goodness of the Lord in the land of the living!" Psalm 27:8, 13 (RSV)

May happiness be yours during this season of goodwill and may the New Year bring peace on Earth. 2001

The 2001 holiday card features the second floor corridor of the White House with Mary Cassatt's 1908 painting, Young Mother and Two Children. *Mrs. Bush selected the psalm for the card on September 16. (White House Archives)*

The gold, red, and green color scheme planned for the 2001 National Christmas Tree was changed after the events of September 11 to reflect a renewed sense of American patriotism, featuring more than 100,000 blue and white lights, red garlands, and oversized white stars. First Lady Laura Bush echoed that patriotic spirit in a special holiday message to the American people, saying: "This year the holiday season holds a special meaning for Americans around the world. The terrorist attacks of September 11 were designed to tear at the fabric of our nation's confidence and spirit. They failed. Instead, Americans of diverse backgrounds are united as never before. We stand shoulder to shoulder behind a flag that stands for freedom, honor, and pride." (*Family Circle Magazine*, December 2001)

(White House Archives)

America seeks peace and believes in justice. We fight only when necessary. We fight so that oppression may cease, and even in the midst of war, we pray for peace on Earth and good will to men.

This is a time of the year for families and friends to gather together, not simply to

In 2003, the Christmas theme, A Season of Stories, *combined the wonder of the season with the magic of classic children's stories that have captured America's hearts and minds for generations. Decorations included Clifford, the Big Red Dog; the Cat in the Hat; the Polar Express; and Harry Potter. (George W. Bush Presidential Library and Museum)*

celebrate the season but to renew the bonds of love and affection that give fulfillment to our lives. And this is a year we will not forget those who lost loved ones in the attacks on September the 11th and on the battlefield. They will remain in our prayers.

It is now my honor to invite Leon Patterson and Faith Elseth and Laura to join me up here as we light the National Christmas Tree. Leon and Faith's fathers, Major Clifford Patterson and Lt. Commander Robert Elseth, served in the United States military. Both of these good men were lost in the attack on the Pentagon.

Leon and Faith, we thank you for helping us celebrate Christmas. You remind us of the comfort of Christmas, that hope never fails and love never ends.

And now, would you please help Laura light up our beautiful tree.

(George W. Bush, "Remarks on Lighting the National Christmas Tree," December 6, 2001.)

President George W. Bush and First Lady Laura Bush pose in the Blue Room prior to hosting a reception for Kennedy Center honorees. (White House Archives)

2009
A Spirit of Unity
BARACK OBAMA

HISTORICAL NOTE: On January 20, 2009, the United States inaugurated its first African-American president, Barack Obama. While many felt that the new administration would help to heal a country divided by its continued involvement in the Iraq War, others were more concerned by a global financial crisis and America's deepest recession since the Great Depression. In his first message at the lighting of the National Christmas Tree, President Obama spoke about the need for unity.

In 1923, the Washington DC public schools wrote a letter to the White House asking if they could put up a Christmas tree on the South Lawn. And First Lady Grace Coolidge said they could use the Ellipse. And in the eight decades since, in times of war and peace,

President Barack Obama and First Lady Michelle Obama pose in front of the White House Christmas tree in the Blue Room. (Official White House Photo)

hardship and joy, Americans from every corner of this Nation have gathered here to share in the holiday spirit.

Tonight we celebrate a story that is as beautiful as it is simple. The story of a child born far from home to parents guided only by faith, but who would ultimately spread a message that has endured for more than 2,000 years, that no matter who we are or where we are from, we are each called to love one another as brother and sister.

While this story may be a Christian one, its lesson is universal. It speaks to the hope we share as a people, and it represents a tradition that we celebrate as a country, a tradition that has come to represent more than any one holiday or religion, but a season of brotherhood and generosity to our fellow citizens.

It's that spirit of unity that we must remember as we light the

National Christmas Tree, a tree that will shine its light far beyond our city and our shores to every American around the world. And that's why tonight our thoughts and prayers are with the men and women who will be spending this holiday far away from home, the mothers and fathers, the sons and daughters of our military who risk their lives every day to keep us safe. We will be thinking of you and praying for you during this holiday season.

President Barack Obama, with mother-in-law Marian Robinson, daughters Sasha and Malia, and First Lady Michelle Obama, react as they push the button to light the National Christmas Tree in 2010. (Official White House Photo)

In 2011, a windstorm containing gusts of up to fifty miles per hour snapped the trunk of the National Christmas Tree which had stood on the Ellipse for over thirty years. A Colorado blue spruce was planted in its stead but died of transplant shock a year later. Another Colorado blue spruce was selected as a replacement and planted less than forty-eight hours before Hurricane Sandy passed near the Washington DC area in 2012. Amazingly, the tree survived the storm and made its debut at the lighting of the National Christmas Tree just one month later.

And let's also remember our neighbors who are struggling here at home, those who've lost a job or a home, a friend or a loved one, because even though it's easy to focus on receiving at this time of year, it's often in the simple act of giving that we find the greatest happiness.

So on behalf of Michelle and Malia and Sasha and my mother-in-law Mama Robinson, I want to wish all of you a very merry Christmas. May you go out with joy and be led forth in peace.

(Barack Obama, "Remarks by the President at the National Christmas Tree Lighting Ceremony," December 3, 2009.)

The 2014 National Christmas Tree on the Ellipse.
(Official White House Photo)

TIMELINE OF U.S. PRESIDENTS

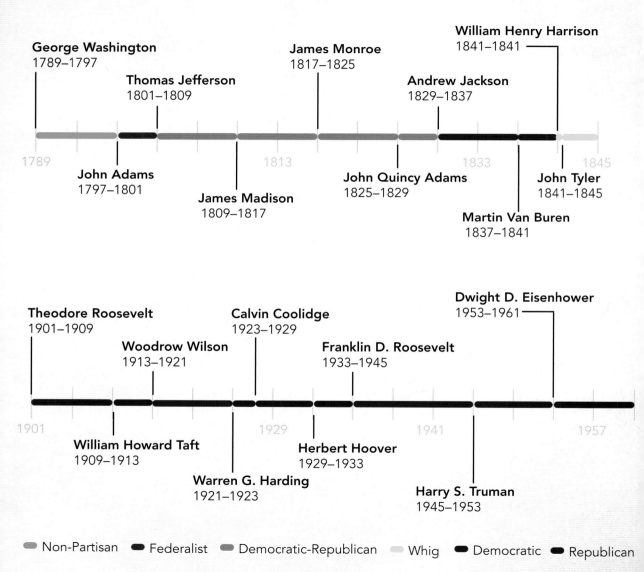

George Washington
1789–1797

Thomas Jefferson
1801–1809

James Monroe
1817–1825

Andrew Jackson
1829–1837

William Henry Harrison
1841–1841

1789

John Adams
1797–1801

James Madison
1809–1817

1813

John Quincy Adams
1825–1829

1833

John Tyler
1841–1845

1845

Martin Van Buren
1837–1841

Theodore Roosevelt
1901–1909

Calvin Coolidge
1923–1929

Dwight D. Eisenhower
1953–1961

Woodrow Wilson
1913–1921

Franklin D. Roosevelt
1933–1945

1901

William Howard Taft
1909–1913

1929

Herbert Hoover
1929–1933

1941

1957

Warren G. Harding
1921–1923

Harry S. Truman
1945–1953

● Non-Partisan ● Federalist ● Democratic-Republican ● Whig ● Democratic ● Republican

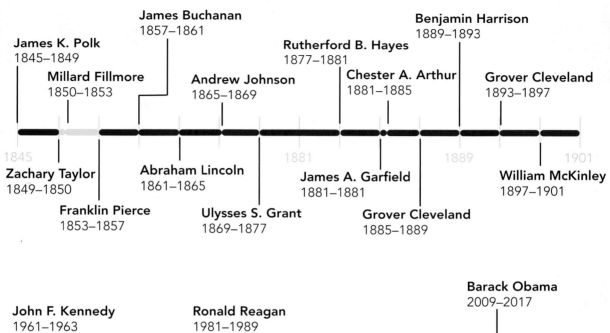

James K. Polk
1845–1849

Millard Fillmore
1850–1853

James Buchanan
1857–1861

Andrew Johnson
1865–1869

Rutherford B. Hayes
1877–1881

Chester A. Arthur
1881–1885

Benjamin Harrison
1889–1893

Grover Cleveland
1893–1897

1845

1881

1889

1901

Zachary Taylor
1849–1850

Franklin Pierce
1853–1857

Abraham Lincoln
1861–1865

Ulysses S. Grant
1869–1877

James A. Garfield
1881–1881

Grover Cleveland
1885–1889

William McKinley
1897–1901

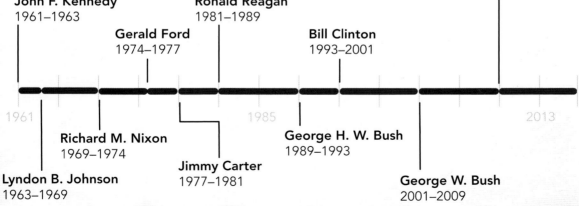

John F. Kennedy
1961–1963

Gerald Ford
1974–1977

Ronald Reagan
1981–1989

Bill Clinton
1993–2001

Barack Obama
2009–2017

1961

1985

2013

Richard M. Nixon
1969–1974

George H. W. Bush
1989–1993

Lyndon B. Johnson
1963–1969

Jimmy Carter
1977–1981

George W. Bush
2001–2009

*The 2002 White House Christmas card showing the National Christmas Tree
and the individual State trees. Painting by Kamil Kubik.
(George W. Bush Presidential Library and Museum)*